# A BROKEN MIND OF A MARINE

Desmond A. Cook

NEWMAN SPRINGS PUBLISHING
320 Broad Street
Red Bank, NJ 07701

First originally published by Newman Springs Publishing 2024

ISBN 979-8-89308-737-6 (Paperback)
ISBN 979-8-89308-738-3 (Digital)

Printed in the United States of America

# Contents

THIS GOES OUT TO THE BRAVE MEN and women who sacrificed on the battlefields and walked the wall so that we could all sleep at night.

All gave some, and some gave ALL. Not all battle wounds are visible.

I Got Your 6 (IGY6).

This book is inspired by true events. This book is filled with strong language and graphic accounts. Some names and events were changed for dramatic effects.

I WAS BORN ON A MONDAY; IT WAS on February 23, 1970, to be exact. I was the youngest child that was born to my mother and father, the third of three. My mother and father were divorced when I was two years old. My mother remarried, and she and my stepfather had a child together—a boy—so technically, I was now number three of four. I was five at the time of his birth. I have an older sister (Lucy), an older brother (Jimmy), and a younger brother (Charlie). My sister Lucy was named after my grandmother; Jimmy was named after my father; and Charlie was named after his father. I'm the only one of the kids who was not named after anyone in the family. I got my name, David, from an actor on TV when my mother was a little girl. Being named David after an actor that my mother was fond of as a little girl made me always feel like there was no way for me to stand out from the rest of the kids in my family because there was no specific family significance attached to my name for it to be memorable to anyone other than my mother.

My mother had a brother named Hank. Since he was younger than my mother but just a few years older than we were, we kind of looked at him as more of an older brother than an uncle. Lucy was a straight "A" student; she was one of those people who thought that if she got a "B," then her life would be over. Jimmy was a natural athlete that could run fast, jump high, and had the physical appearance of someone that could easily be perceived as probably being able to lift an entire house from its foundation without breaking a sweat. On the other hand, I was a C student, and as far as sports, I had to work very hard just to be average. I never really wanted to be an athlete, but because Jimmy was one, all the coaches thought I was too. The teachers all thought that because Lucy was a straight "A" student, I would be a straight "A" student as well. I guess the teachers and coaches were surprised when I came around because I was nothing like my brother or sister. Was I a disappointment…even to myself? Once again, I was not like the other kids.

As a kid, I always wanted to hang out with Jimmy and Hank, but they never let me, saying that I was too young and a pain in the ass. That always made me mad, so I would do things to irritate them that would make them mad. In return, they would beat me up. For me, that was a good thing because when they beat me up, that meant that they had to spend time with me to do so. I can remember one time I made Hank and Jimmy so mad that Jimmy held me down, and Hank took a hot iron and branded me on the butt with it. The average kid, heck, the average adult, would have thought twice about bothering those two anymore; obviously, I'm not the average person. Little did they know that all of those beatings they gave me were forming a very soon-to-be dark-sided man.

After taking so many beatings, it felt normal to have pain coursing through my body. It got to the point where I started to enjoy the pain. To feel that pain, I was actually doing things that would cause me pain—yes, I started inflicting pain on myself and later found that my actions were actually a form of mental illness. To me, pain was a way to let me know that I was alive. One of the things that I would do was stick things into the outlets to get shocked. I wanted to see how long I could take the pain of the electricity flowing through my body. I'm talking about someone who is like nine years old. I knew that I enjoyed the pain because it made me feel alive. Not all pain was the same, but all pain made me feel alive. I thought that maybe others also enjoyed pain. Am I truly that different?

To prove my point, I first started with a cat. I took that cat and choked it till I could see the life fade from its eyes. I let it go, then I did it again, and this time I did not let go! I'm sure that I could feel the soul of that cat seep into my hands. I kind of liked the way it felt when that life went into me. I killed a few cats, but that was not enough. I needed to see if, by killing something bigger than a cat, I would feel more of that energy flowing into me. I then killed a dog with my hands and also killed one with a baseball bat. The one that I killed with a bat was not as pleasing as the one that was killed by hand. The one by hand took longer, but I could feel the life draining from it. I have killed many things, from birds to a cow. The only thing about the cow was it was too big to kill by hand, but a well-placed bullet would drop a cow.

Understand something; to me, it was never about torturing anything. To me, in the beginning, it was all about seeing if others liked pain as much as I did. That first time that I killed something, it was no longer about seeing if pain was liked; it was about the feeling of life making its way into my body. All of that was before I was seventeen years old. I often wondered what it would be like to feel the life of a man seeping into my body. I imagined killing a man would be more complex than killing an animal. Animals are easy; grab them and kill them. The thing about killing a man is that you have to plan exactly how you will kill him. You would then need to plan for any unexpected accidents. Like, what if someone saw us, what if he got away, what if he has a weapon, etc. The list of what-ifs is endless. It is becoming clear that, no, I am not like everyone else. I had a cousin that I was able to talk into killing someone with me…

My cousin and I chose a person and planned how we were going to do this. On the east end of the city that I lived in, there were some old railroad tracks that ran behind a bar. We knew that often drunks would walk the tracks on their way home. So one night, my cousin and I waited in the dark for one of those drunks walking the tracks. We must have waited hours, or at least it felt like hours, for someone to walk into our trap. The longer we waited for someone to stagger by, the more anxious I became. My hands were sweating, almost like I was running them underwater. I strained to see shapes in the darkness, so it made me a little jittery every time I heard a sound. I could tell that my cousin wanted to turn back and not go through with it.

I could visibly see that he was nervous. I wasn't sure if he was going to run or stay. I could feel myself starting to get angry, thinking that he was going to run and leave me to do this on my own. When some drunken bastard made it to our trap, we pounced on him like two wild Rottweilers. He was a big bastard and put up one hell of a fight, but in the end, we won the fight and beat him to death. The way he fought for his last breath was exhilarating. I think that he knew that his life was almost over. It is amazing how hard a person will fight when they think that they're in the fight of their life; the will to live kicks in. That's when your heart starts to race, you can hear every beat of your heart, your lips start to tingle, your vision becomes focused, your legs are shaky, and your hands are sweaty. At least that's what I was feeling.

I believe that man sobered up very quickly after about the second hit that he took. It took two hits to put him down, but he bounced back up very quickly. When he got back to his feet, he asked, "What the hell?" We said nothing to him; we just started toward him. I'm not sure who was more nervous, the man or me. He was nervous because he knew that he was in the fight of his life, and I was nervous because my cousin looked like he was about to run. I wasn't sure if I could have taken him by myself, but I knew that there was no turning back. This was it, because I may never get this chance again! We were two seventeen-year-old boys killing a grown man. It wasn't quite as I thought it would be.

I wanted to feel his life seep into my body, so I told my cousin that I wanted to do it again. I think that it may have been too much for my cousin to handle because he said that he was done and that if I wanted to do it again, then I was on my own. He said that he couldn't sleep for days afterward. He said that every time he closed his eyes, he could hear that guy screaming and begging for his life. He also talked about how hard it was to wash that guy's blood off his hands. He said that he thinks he washed his hands about thirty times before he was able to get all the blood off. I felt bad for my cousin after that happened because he was never the same after that night.

Plus, we were no longer as close as we had been. I could just be wrong, but I also think that he looked at and treated me differently after that night. It was almost as if just being around me frightened him. I would come over to see him and ask if he wanted to go places with me, and he would come up with excuses as to why he couldn't go; most of the time I knew that he was full of shit.

I knew that doing it again was something that I wanted or even needed to do. I even wrote about it in school. In my civics class, we had to write a paper on what we wanted to do when we grew up. Not only did we have to write a paper, but we also had to stand up in front of the class to read our papers and answer any questions that the class may have. My paper was about being a hitman. I told them how I would kill my clients. Some of the ways that I talked about was making a bullet out of dry ice so that when I shoot someone, the bullet melts and will never be traced back to me. Or how about having two big, mean dogs and sick them on the client and just stepping into the crowd and watching the dogs mangle the client.

The police comes to kill the dogs that killed the person; all evidence dies with the dogs. I even talked about ramming an ice cycle through the eye and into the brain of a client. The cycle melts again, and so does the evidence. Obviously, we all know that you could never make a bullet out of dry ice and fire it from a gun. The ice would melt before ever leaving the chamber. Of course, as a child, you don't know those things. But you have to admit that it was pretty creative…I am definitely not like everyone else.

# Jody

I KNEW THAT I WAS MEANT TO GO into the military at an early age. Being in the military meant that I might get the chance to kill someone and get away with it. The military kills people all the time. I believed the best branch to join would be the Marines. They have a reputation for being badasses. So being a Marine, I knew I would get the chance that I was looking for. So at the age of eighteen, on the sixteenth of January, I left for Parris Island, South Carolina, Marine Corps Boot Camp to become a United States Marine.

Boot camp was everything that I thought it would be. Most people considered boot camp a mental game, but not me. To me, it was a place that would allow me to perform that sought-after kill. The Marines explained about killing and how to kill. I knew that I had found my place! In boot camp, you were punished for everything you did, right or wrong. This mental testing did not faze me. I was completely in my element.

The Marine Corps drill instructors were the potters, and the recruits were considered the clay. They wanted to break you down and rebuild you as a lean, mean fighting machine, which came easy for me. I loved to fight. The more they punished me, the more I enjoyed boot camp. They could not break me down to make me a killing machine because that was done long before I ever joined the

Marines. It only enhanced the way that I felt inside. My longing to absorb other human souls was heightened.

The Marines fed the monster hiding inside of me that was starving for the soul of a man. Those thirteen weeks that I spent in boot camp made that monster famished! After those thirteen weeks were over, I went home on leave and found that my girlfriend (Franchesca) was messing around on me while I was at training. The funny thing is that in boot camp, the drill instructors used that as motivation to make us angry enough to want to kill! They would always tell us, "That Jody got your girl and gone." (Jody is the name of the guy that took your girl.)

Every time they would talk about Jody, I would think that if I ever came across Jody, I would kill him and enjoy it. Many times I had a dream that I came home and found Jody with my girlfriend (Franchesca). Each time I had that dream, I killed Jody differently. I think I must have wished this to fruition. I was a bit excited to find that Jody had been messing with my girl while I was gone. But Jody was not Jody; his name was Ben.

I knew Ben from long ago. He was the guy who was my sister's first boyfriend and tried to force himself on her. When that happened, I was just a kid, and there was nothing that I could do about it. Lucy never told our mother what happened to her. The only way I found out was that I overheard her tell a friend about it. So that was one more reason that Ben should die. I told my girlfriend Franchesca to take me to Jody, she looked at me as if I had two heads. Then she asked me who Jody was. I looked at her and said, "The motherfucker that you were laying with while I was at boot camp." First, she looked me in the eyes and lied to me, saying that she was not with anyone while I was away! I told her that I was going to kill Jody.

She said I don't know a Jody. I told her Jody was Ben, and her eyes looked like they were going to pop out of her head. She asked how I knew about Ben, and I told her that people saw them together. She said that they were just friends and didn't do anything. I asked her if she thought that I was stupid. She tried to convince me that they were never together. The rage in me grew!

I looked her in the eyes and told her that I would twist her freaking neck till her head popped off if she kept lying to me. I think that she saw in my eyes that I would have done it. She started to cry and told me that she was sorry and that he didn't mean anything to her. At that point, I'm not sure if I cared if he did or didn't. The only thing I could think of was stomping his head in until his brain came gushing out. I wanted to see if you could stomp someone's head with that much force. The drill instructor who taught hand-to-hand combat said that it was totally possible. Franchesca took me to the home of a guy named Tony. I asked her how the hell she knew that he was at Tony's.

I knew she was going to lie to me, so I stopped her before she could say anything. I knocked on the door, and who should answer the door but Ben! I told Ben that I was there to kill him for messing with my girlfriend when I was in boot camp. Ben stepped back from the door with a look in his eyes, like he was about to piss in his pants. I could hear my drill instructor's voice in my head telling me what to do to Jody. I started to smile. When I started to smile, I think it must have confused Ben. Thinking back on it, what kind of person tells you that they're there to kill you for being with their girlfriend, then starts to smile afterward? He started to look relieved and even started to smile, until I slapped him in the face.

The slap echoed throughout the house and made his lip bleed. I thought that he would have hit me back, but he didn't. Instead, he looked at Tony and asked him if he was going to let this go down in his house. Tony stood up and said, "You need to get the fuck out of my crib with the bullshit." I looked at Tony and told him to suck my dick! I stepped toward Ben, and he begged me to leave him alone. He said that he was only with her because she said that she was not with anyone. Tony came into the hallway, where we were standing with his gun, and told me to get the fuck out of his crib. I looked at Tony and told him to shoot me because I can't die; I'm a Marine!

That was something that was taught to us in boot camp. Marines are indestructible. That's when Ben saw his chance and ran out of the back door. I knew Tony wasn't going to use his gun on me; he couldn't look me in the eyes, plus he still had the safety on. I pushed past him and ran after Ben. I don't think that I've ever seen anyone run that fast before. I'm sure that I chased Ben for about a mile, toying with him like a cat would a mouse. Calling out to Ben with every step that I took, and every time he turned around, I smiled. "Ben, I'm coming for you, Ben." I could have caught him long before I did, but I enjoyed the chase and the fear that he felt, knowing I would catch up to him.

The entire time that I was chasing Ben, he was yelling for someone to help him. Someone must have heard him yelling that I was trying to kill him. Just as I caught him, the police pulled up. The officer got out of his car and asked what was going on. Ben said that I was trying to kill him. The officer looked me up and down. I'm sure that he was wondering why I was dressed the way that I was. I was dressed in my gold PT (Physical Training) t-shirt with USMC in red letters across the chest, my camo pants bloused in my black boots. The officer asked me if I was in the Marines, and I said, "Sir, yes, sir. I just got home from boot camp last night."

He asked where I went to boot camp, and I said, "Sir, Parris Island, sir; platoon 2025, second battalion Hotel Company." He smiled and said that he went to Parris Island also and that he was in the third battalion. Then he asked me what was going on. I looked at him, pointed to Ben, and told him that Ben was Jody. The officer looked at Ben with disgust in his eyes. Ben said that his name was not Jody; it was Ben, and that he was not sure why I was trying to kill him. The officer asked him if he was with my girlfriend when I was away in boot camp. Ben had a puzzled look on his face. Ben still didn't answer. The officer turned to me and said, "Devil dog, as much as I would love to sit and watch you stomp his grape in, I unfortunately can't do that."

The officer looked at Ben and said that he would keep me there till he had time to run away. Ben stood there looking confused, and the officer said you better get moving before I get in my car, pull away, and leave you two to talk about this. Ben was gone in a flash. The officer stood and talked to me for a bit longer. He asked me what my MOS (Military Occupational Specialty) was. I told him it was 7222 (Hawk Missiles). He told me that his MOS was 0311

(Infantry). I told him that's what I wanted, and my recruiter said that I didn't want that. My recruiter was 0311 and said that as soon as he got back to the fleet, he was going to switch to something else.

He told me to go on an open contract. Little did I know that if you go on an open contract, they will look at your test scores and place you where they need you. The higher your score, the more technical job they give you. The officer told me good luck, got in his car, and drove away. I ran back to Tony's, hoping that Ben would go back to his house.

Ben never went, so I got in the car with Franchesca and left. I spent about a week at home and left for Alabama for my MOS school. Before I left to go to Alabama, I broke up with Franchesca. I told her to enjoy her time with Ben. My thoughts were a new beginning and a new life. My focus was on being a Marine. So for the next six months, I put all of my concentration on learning about the Hawk missile. Was my focus shifting from killing to being one of the few and proud? Perhaps…

# First Duty Station

Now I am a full-fledged Marine. My first duty station is in Japan. After six months in Japan, the Marine Corps said that they were doing away with the Hawk missiles and that I needed to find a new job. Also around that time, I reconnected with my ex-girlfriend, Franchesca. I even went back to the States to marry her. Before I left to go back to the States to marry Franchesca, I submitted my paperwork to go to STA Platoon (Surveillance and Target Acquisition).

I got back to Japan, and my first sergeant called me into his office and told me to go pack my shit. I wasn't sure why he was telling me to pack my shit. That's not something you want to hear your first sergeant say to you. The first sergeant wasn't a very big man in size but commanded respect as if he were a thirty-foot-tall giant. The first sergeant was one of those Marines left over from Vietnam. Rumors had it that the first sergeant was a tunnel rat in Nam (someone that goes in the tunnels after the Viet Cong with nothing more than a flashlight and a 45-cal. pistol). It was said that the first sergeant volunteered to do that job, so when the first sergeant said to jump, you just jumped and stayed in the air till he said to come down.

So I looked at the first sergeant and swallowed hard, then said, "First sergeant, may I ask why I have to pack my stuff?" I wasn't sure if I should be asking him that question, but I couldn't help myself because I had to know. He looked up from the papers on his desk at me. I was sure that he was going to rip my head off my neck and use it as a pencil holder. He just smiled at me, and I wasn't sure what to do. I was confused because I had never seen him smile before. I'm sure that I saw parts of his face crack off and fall onto his desk. I'm sure that was the first time that he had smiled in years. He told me that he had pulled some strings and got me into STA Platoon.

He also told me not to step on my dick because he was at one time in STA Platoon and held it close to his heart. The first sergeant told me to report to the S-2 (intelligence) OIC (officer in charge). I said, "Roger that first sergeant," and ran from his office. Now that I got into STA Platoon, I had to change my MOS to 0311 (Infantry). That was a dream come true for me, because that's what I wanted from the beginning. STA Platoon Marines are high-speed, low-drag, hard chargers that are specially trained for close-range reconnaissance and information gathering for the battalion commander. They work in small teams (three to four men) employing ground surveillance radar and night observation devices to aid the battalion commander in locating the enemy at the forward edge of the battle area. Scout snipers are also a part of STA Platoon, so if you go out in a three- or four-man team, one of them is normally a scout sniper. This excited me because it meant that I might get the chance to kill someone. The monster was still there. Maybe even get to take a shot using a sniper rifle and send a round down range and in the middle of someone's head.

There are two kinds of Marines in STA Platoon: the PIGs (Professionally Instructed Gunmen) and the HOGs (Hunter of Gunmen). HOGs are school-trained snipers, and PIGs are taught by the HOGs throughout their time in STA Platoon. All the time that I was packing, all I could think about was that I felt like a little kid who just got everything that he asked for at Christmas.

I reported to the OIC of S-2 for reassignment into STA Platoon. Most of my training was OJT (On-the-Job Training). Shortly after going over to STA Platoon, I got a set of orders to Cubi Point, Subic Bay, Philippines. The orders were for JEST (Jungle Environment Survival Training). Just like the name says, it was jungle survival skills like building shelters from natural materials, moving through the thick vegetation or across the water, and procuring food and water from nature. When I got to JEST, I saw that it was more than just Marines that attended this school. It was for all branches of the military, plus other countries. I was surprised to see some of the people who showed up for this school. Officers and enlisted were in this course together.

From the first day to the last day of class, we were in the jungle. I remember the first time we ate something in the course; it was from a large table that was in the middle of the room. You had to go around and take a little of everything from each dish on the table and eat it. The next day, I remember getting something to eat and going back into that room with the big table, but this time all of the dishes were labeled. Like monkeys, snakes, snails, tree bark, and so on. Everything about this course turned me on. In my mind, they were just making me a better and stronger killer, one that could kill on the streets as well as in the jungle. We were wet, dirty, and drained every day, but I always had a smile on my face. To me, this was just an investment, and the payoff in the end was having more opportunities and skills to take a life.

This course was mentally and physically fatiguing, but more so for those who were not in top physical condition. The washout rate for this course is about 30–40 percent. That means that 30–40 percent of the people who came to the course left without a certificate of completion. I would have hung myself from a tree with a vine until I was dead before I went back to my unit and told them that I was a bitch and couldn't do it.

The last day of the course, I was back on a plane on my way back to Japan. On my way back to "The sharp edge of the sword" that's what we called ourselves. "The sharp edge of the sword" that has to be the coolest freaking saying in the world. We all know that the sharp edge of the sword is the best and deadliest part of the sword. Shortly after I got back to my unit in Japan, I got orders to go back to the States. My time in Japan was over, and now I had orders to go to the second Marine Davion H&S (Headquarters and Service) Battalion Camp Lejeune, NC.

I was excited that I was back in the States and to be with my new wife. We could now start our lives together because, a few days after we were married, I had to go back to Japan. I thought that we had a great life together, but Franchesca must have thought differently. I only say that because shortly after I got home from Japan, I had to go away to California for about six months for training. Three months into the training, Franchesca called to tell me that she was pregnant. At first, I was excited until something told me to ask her how far along she was. So I asked her how far along she was, and her silence was deafening. So I asked her a second time.

This time she answered me and said that she was one month pregnant. I paused for a minute and said, "Can you please explain to me how you can be one month pregnant if I've been gone three months." I just said that we would talk about it when I got home and hung up the phone. I told my sergeant what my wife had just told me, and he asked me if I wanted to go home early to take care of it. I told him that I would deal with it when I got back home.

A few days later, my sergeant told me that he had talked to the lieutenant, and the two of them felt I should go home early. Before they let me go home, they expressed to me several times that if I went home and killed my wife or her boyfriend, I would go to prison. I knew that I could not go home and do anything to them, no matter how much I wanted to. I was cool about the situation when I got home. The plane ride from California back to North Carolina was a long ride for me because I wasn't sure how things would go. I knew how I wanted them to go. I played our conversation in my head, over and over. I didn't tell her that they were sending me home early; I wanted it to be a surprise. I was the one who was surprised, because he was at the house when I got home.

I wanted so badly to do something to him, but I didn't. I told him that he needed to leave so that my wife and I could talk. As he was leaving, it took everything in me not to do something to him. She and I sat down to talk about what we were going to do next. My suggestion was that she have the baby, I sign the birth certificate, we tell everyone that it is my kid, and she never talks to him ever again. She said that wouldn't be fair to him, so I suggested that she have the baby, give it to him, and never see him again. She said that wouldn't be fair to her. So my last suggestion was that she get the hell out and be with him. The funny thing is, this suggestion was one that she could live with.

The night that she left, all I felt was anger and rage. I felt that she had robbed me. She knew that I wanted nothing more in life than to have a family of my own. That is all that we talked about, and now she is taking that dream from me. She took my dream and gave it to someone else. How could she do something like that to me? That night I went for a drive. I was driving around and came across a prostitute. I picked up the prostitute and found out that the woman, so I thought, was a man. This made me even angrier and filled me with even more rage. Before I knew what happened, I had my hands around her or his neck. The harder she or he fought, the harder I squeezed her or his neck. I strangely felt joy and peace after choking her or him to death.

I can't say if it's because my wife just left me or that I was feeding that monster that lived deep inside me. Whatever the reason was that I did what I did, I don't know, but what I do know is that it felt good and I liked it. Yes, I was different from other people. Was my most recent kill due to rage and heartache caused by my wife's indiscretion? Was my monster simply lying in wait for my next opportunity to feed him?

# Operation Desert Storm

Shortly after my encounter with the prostitute, I learned about a guy whose name was Saddam Hussein. He was the dictator of the country of Iraq. On August 2, 1990, Santa, using the name of Saddam Hussein, brought me a very special gift. The special gift was a war. Saddam Hussein, at that time, decided to invade Kuwait. Saddam was a war-hungry bastard. He had just ended an eight-year war with the country of Iran. Saddam set his sights on the country of Kuwait. At that time, Kuwait was the smallest but richest country in the Middle East. Within a few hours after attacking, Saddam overran the entire country of Kuwait.

As I watched this unfold on TV, I knew it wouldn't be long before we went over to help. On August 10, 1990, we had a company formation, and the company commander told us that we had three days to get all of our affairs in order because we had orders coming down to ship out. He didn't tell us where we were going, but we all knew it had something to do with Iraq invading Kuwait. After the formation, I was walking on air, thinking that my time was coming. I was on top of the world; my wife was back, and I'm going to war.

When I got home, I made love to my wife like I never had before. The thought of going off to war was the best aphrodisiac ever! Just think I will get the chance not to just kill one, but to kill many and not have to answer for my actions. I just kept saying thank you, Saddam, over and over, because he gave me a great gift, and he didn't even know. I thought to myself that you just unleashed a hungry monster on your people. A monster that has a giant appetite and needs to be fed. A monster that, when finally freed, will destroy everything in its path. A monster that once let off the leash may never be able to be put back on the leash. I'm sure that I wasn't the only one thinking that way. Could you imagine letting thousands of men who think like I do loose? Hundreds of hungry monsters looking to feed off the souls of other men. I couldn't imagine a greater picture than seeing all of those hungry monsters feeding on the battlefield.

On August 14, 1990, we were on a plane on the way to Egypt. That had to be the longest trip of my life. I felt like a little kid the day before Christmas. I couldn't sleep. All I could think about was how soon it would be before me and Ms. Kitty were on the battlefield, collecting souls. Ms. Kitty is the name that I gave to my rifle. That was something that came from boot camp, naming your rifle. Ms. Kitty was also just as excited as I was to get started on our mission. Our mission was to see how many souls we would be able to collect.

When our plane was landing in Egypt, I didn't know what to expect, but I had a funny feeling inside. You know that feeling when you are nervous plus excited? Well, that's what I was feeling inside. The airplane hit the runway and skidded to a stop. When the doors opened up and the heated air rushed into the plane, it felt as if it had punched me in the face. It was like a wake-up call, saying you're here. My palms were starting to get sweaty, and my legs felt a little shaky. I'm ready to go! The only thing I could think of is like in the movies, when they step off the plane, rounds are coming at them, and they are just shooting in the direction that they think the rounds are coming from.

As I'm making my way to the door, I'm getting more and more excited. I step out of the plane, and all I see is the airport and the buses at the foot of the ladder that they have against the plane for us to ride in. I felt let down, almost like you've been waiting to go on a date with the most beautiful woman you've ever met, knowing at the end of the night you're going to have sex with her in every way possible under the sun. She even made some comments, making you think that something was definitely going to happen. So far, the date is going like you expected, and now the date is over. You're driving her back to her place rock hard, and can't wait. Now that you're at her place, walk her up to her front door, and she gives you a kiss on the cheek and says, "*I'll call you.*" That's how I felt when all I saw was the runway and buses! I looked at Ms. Kitty and said, "I'm sorry, baby. Maybe next time."

I walked down the ladder and got on the bus, not sure if I was disappointed or pissed off. This was by far the biggest disappointment I've ever had. It was a long bus ride to get to the base that we were staying at. The ride was about an hour away from the airport, but it had to be the longest damn hour ever. We got to our command base, squared away our gear, and did the thing that every Marine hates to do…hurry up and wait! It's exactly how it sounds; hurry up and wait! It just means that you sit and do nothing. For the first few days, we did nothing, which was mostly to help us acclimate to the weather. In the second week, we start to train on the terrain alongside troops from other countries. After training with some of these other countries, you say to yourself, no wonder you lost the war because you fucking suck.

Weeks go by, and these weeks turn into months. Ms. Kitty and I are starting to get pissed off. We felt like we were being teased every day that we were here, not in gauging in taking a life. January 10, 1990, at 0200 hours (2:00 a.m.), under the cover of the night, the freaking trucks rolled out. I knew that we were going to fulfill our mission. I can't tell you where we set up camp, but I can tell you that I was more excited than I had ever been in my life.

For the next few days that we were in Saudi Arabia, we went over our battle plans. January 16, 1990, at 0100 hours, I heard the first boom from a plane dropping its load. That means that the war has officially started. The only thing I could think of is game on now, baby. I took out my special rag that I used to keep Ms. Kitty clean and started to wipe her down so that when we got our invite to the dance, she would be the prettiest girl at the ball. That first boom was the beginning of a massive US-led air offensive that rained hell down on the Iraqi troops that occupied Kuwait. This was also the beginning of Operation Desert Storm.

So for the next forty-two glory days, it was a relentless attack from the air and on the ground by the coalition forces. Our first mission was to take back the American Embassy that had fallen under the control of the Iraqis. I remember there was a hotel across the street from it. I can't remember the name of the hotel. The first thing that we did when we got to the hotel was to go floor by floor and clear the hotel so that we could have the high ground when we took back the Embassy.

After taking the hotel, I was posted in a window facing the front of the Embassy, and one of the sergeants told me to set up Big Betty and ride her. Big Betty was a nasty bitch. She was a .50 caliber (12.7mm) link-belt-fed air-cooled machine gun that could spit out seven hundred fifty to eight hundred rounds per minute. Just think, that's about fourteen rounds a second coming at you with no place to hide because Big Betty doesn't play! She can reach out and touch you from a mile away. Don't even think about hiding behind a wall because she has been known to spit through a brick wall. You don't want to piss Big Betty off because, like I said, "She is one mean bitch and loves to show off."

I had a bit of a struggle going on inside of me because I came to the dance with Ms. Kitty, and now I had to lay her aside for Big Betty. But how could you say no to Big Betty? Don't get me wrong, I loved Ms. Kitty, but Big Betty is what wet dreams are made of. I also knew that with me riding Big Betty, I would not be a part of the ground forces rushing the Embassy. On the other hand, with me ridding Big Betty, I was like a god and could fuck some shit up. Raining down hellfire on those mother fuckers below. Watching them looking into the sky as if they were praying to me to stop the hellfire that was raining on their heads. After setting up Big Betty, I felt like a virgin about to have sex for the first time. I couldn't wait for the order to go hot.

I just kept talking to Big Betty, telling her that we were going to have a good time at this dance and that if she does right by me, then I'll do right by her. Together, we'll have some fun! We had a loudspeaker set up and blasting it out of one of the broken windows for them to put their weapons down, hands up, and come out. We repeated the same message for about ten minutes straight. Then my sergeant told me to put a few rounds over the front wall and into the courtyard. I think I put about ten rounds down in the courtyard, then we repeated the message. After that, we started taking fire from the Embassy. We got the order to go hot, and I got an instant erection.

I went hot, and Big Betty started spitting brimstone hellfire down below. She started spitting so fast that her barrel started to glow red hot! The person beside me was yelling for me to stop before I melted the barrel. So I grabbed the mitt, unscrewed that barrel, and put the new one on. Talking to myself to make sure I do it the right way. Big Betty was a very picky girl. If her barrel wasn't right, she would either protest and do nothing or blow her stack. I said to myself, remember to screw the barrel all the way on, then back three clicks, so that's what I did. The fight for the Embassy didn't last very long; once they saw that they were outmatched, it was over. The sad thing was that it was the only firefight that we were in. Sadly to say, that wasn't the last time that we took fire. The next time we took fire was by friendly fire. (Friendly fire is by your own people).

We had just moved out into the desert and set up a hasty camp. About a mile down from us was a listening post observation post (LP-OP). We had no idea that it was there, and they had no idea who we were. All they knew was that an Iraqi tank company was headed their way. We had gotten the same message, so we started to dig in. All of a sudden, we heard a loud whistle and a boom, then sand and dirt were raining down on our heads. That fucking LP-OP called in fire on us. They freaking called in fire on their own people! Our radio man was on the line, trying to halt the artillery rounds from dropping on us. The rounds stopped after what seemed like hours, but it was only a few short minutes.

After all was said and done, we were putting twelve Marines in body bags. The crazy thing is that not one of us had fallen in the fight for the Embassy, but twelve of us had fallen to friendly fire. That happened a lot, casualties due to friendly fire. This was the first war in a very long time that the allied coalition forces fought together. So all of these countries brought their new toys to show off. Unfortunately, none of them thought about sharing this information with each other. So when someone spotted a new kind of vehicle that they had never seen before, they would light it up. All of these so-called great leaders, and no one thought this would be a problem before all of these brave men were killed? We had twice the casualties and deaths from friendly fire than from enemy fire.

Our new mission was to find units and collect their Enemy Prisoner of War (EPWs). Once we collected their EPWs, we took them to the US. Army prisoner holding camp. The Marines are not equipped to take care of EPWs; we're the smallest of all the forces. Our mission as Marines is to go in first and take the objective, then the Army comes behind us and occupies that objective as we keep going forward. The Army keeps the enemy from coming back and retaking that objective. So we're not big enough to run an enemy prisoner camp. I can remember we had come across a British unit, and somehow we were talked into taking their EPWs. I'm not sure how that happened because they had their own place for their EPWs.

We took ten EPWs from them: two officers and eight enlisted. When you have officers and enlisted, you keep them apart, so the two officers I put in a connex box (metal shipping container), and the other eight we tied together in a circle. Not thinking about it, but it gets pretty hot in the desert. Add a big metal box with the door shut, and you can guess the rest. Imagine putting a chicken in the oven, and you get what happened. A few days later, when we remembered that they were in there and opened the doors, the first thing that came to mind was that they smelled like chicken. I started laughing so hard that I was crying.

Someone came over to see what I was laughing about, and when I showed them, they didn't think it was as funny as I thought. So I just closed the door, and we moved out, leaving them in there. Like I said earlier, we only had forty-two wonderful days to get some. My birthday fell within those forty-two days, and all I wanted for my birthday was to be in a firefight. That did not happen. Not only did that not happen, but also just five days after my birthday on February

28, 1990, President George H. W. Bush called for a ceasefire. That was the end of the war, so we went from Operation Desert Storm to Operation Desert Shield.

Our missions changed. We were no longer battle-hardened killers. We're now babysitters. I spent the next year of my life playing babysitter in Kuwait. Finally, we got our orders to go back home. All that was left was to clean all of our vehicles and equipment. We had to make sure that all of the sand was cleaned off because the bugs that lived in that sand would cause problems in the states. This was the biggest pain in the ass because everything had to be inspected before it was good to go. We washed those freaking trucks like ten times. The crazy thing is that we left most of those vehicles there, not just us, the Marines, but everyone! After our vehicles passed and we got to the airport and went through customs, the only thing left was to get on the plane and go home.

Our plane landed, and as we were getting our stuff together to get on the plane, our commanding officer told us to stand down. He told us that an order came down saying that all of the reservists had to go home first. We all thought this was bullshit because we had been there for over a year and they had been there for months. To make it even worse, they said that we had to get trained to do customs and work customs as these fuckers were taking our plane home. So for the next three months, we watched plane after plane take off and we were not on any of them.

Our day came, and back to the States we went. It was nice being home, but after having Ms. Kitty with me all day every day and now having to give her up and only seeing her when I checked her out of the armory, it was hard. I was missing her more than I missed my wife when I was away.

The first few months at home were hard; I craved that excitement that I felt over there. I would do things like go to clubs and start fights with the biggest guys in the club. The bigger they were or the worse the odds of me winning, the better it was. One night when I was at the club looking for a fight, I met a Marine who told me if I liked to fight, then I should come down to the snake pit on base.

I asked him what in the heck the snake pit was. He told me it was the boxing gym. I thought this could be a good thing. I can hurt people and not get into any trouble for it. I started thinking, *why don't more people join the Marines? You can kill people on the battlefield, then come home and beat people in the ring. How could life get any better?*

Is my "normal" so different from everyone else? Doesn't everyone have some sort of murderous monster inside them?

# The Snake Pit

From the first time that I walked into the snake pit, I knew that I had found a home away from home. When I put the gloves on for the first time, it was as exciting as being with a woman for the first time. The first time that I was in the ring and hit someone, I thought that I was going to have an orgasm. The look that was on the guy's face when I hit him, I will never forget. This was different than any street fight that I had ever been in. Whenever I was in a street fight, I don't really remember any of it. All I could remember was the start of the fight, and the end of the fight but nothing in between. Boxing, on the other hand, was different.

You watch every hit land, every reaction of the other guy after being hit. This brought me more pleasure than a street fight ever could! I was good at what I did in the ring. After about my tenth fight, the coach asked me if I would be willing to join the Marine Corps boxing team. I looked at him like a puppy, with their head tilted to the side, and said that I thought that I was already on the boxing team. He explained that I could join the team full-time, and that would be my only job. I asked that coach if he was fucking with me, and he said no. I told the coach that I was all in with this, and what did I need to do to make it happen? He gave me the paperwork to fill out and to have my company commander sign off on it. Things looked like they were looking up for me.

My wife came back to me, and now I have the opportunity to box. I was so excited when I went home that night and told my wife that I had made the boxing team. It was like telling her that I won the lottery. I was assigned to the boxing team for the next two years. By the end of those two years, I was twelve and three (12 wins and 3 losses) with nine KO's (knockouts) and went from two hundred twenty pounds to two hundred and sixty pounds. This was from a lot of hard work and a needle. Back then, I didn't know that these same needles that made me bigger and stronger also made me angrier and more aggressive. In my world, aggression was a good thing. Little did I know that what I thought was a good thing was setting me up for failure and a big fall.

My aggression was getting worse. My assignment to the boxing team was over, and I had no way to feed the monster that I had deep inside of me. So I went back to doing what I did best: fighting in the streets. This time I was better at it because now I was trained to be a better fighter. All that changed one night, when at a club, I got into a fight and almost killed the guy. The only thing that kept me from killing him was my wife jumping in to stop me. I was in such a fit of rage that I almost punched my wife in the face. The look she had when she thought that I was going to hit her will haunt me for the rest of my life. That's when I knew that the only place where I belonged was in combat. A few years passed, and my wife and I split for good. It was the best thing for both of us. What I wanted out of life was not what she wanted. You can't force love!

# A New Life

New Beginnings...I found a new girlfriend named Annie. After a few months with Annie, I was sure that she wasn't the right person for me, so I told her that I didn't think that it was working out with us. That's when Annie said that she was pregnant. I was so happy that I forgot that I wanted to end things. I took her to the doctor, and they said that she wasn't pregnant. I was crushed, and it felt like a ton of bricks fell on me. All I could think of was the second time I was robbed of my family. Why did this keep happening to me? Was I that evil of a person that I could not have one thing that I wanted? I stayed with her for about one more month, and one night I could not sleep because I knew that the next morning I was going to tell her that we were done.

That next morning, Annie woke me up with something in her hands. It was a pregnancy test. The test was positive! We went to the doctor, and they said that she was pregnant. I took her home to her apartment, dropped her off, and went to the mall to buy a ring. I didn't tell her that I was buying a ring; I wanted it to be a surprise. I wanted to show her that she gave me the greatest gift I have had.

I called and told my mother what was going on. She told me not to marry her because she was just trying to trap me. I told my mother that this was a sign from God that she and I should be together. How could it not be? All of the other women that I've been with have never gotten pregnant before. My mother, being a devoted Christian, said she was not a sign from God. She is a woman with a kid living in government apartments, looking for a way out of them.

To me, it didn't matter because for once, I created a life and felt just as much, if not more, pleasure as I did whenever I took a life. We got married and had a boy named David. So now I had a wife, a daughter (her daughter), Anna, and a son, David. What more could I ask for? For the first time in a very long time, that monster inside of me was quiet. Life was good! Life was great!

Three years passed, and we had another child. A beautiful little girl named Destiny. Now, life was perfect until the day that Annie betrayed me. She put someone outside of our family before me. This woke the monster back up. Once the monster was awakened from his long nap, he was hungrier than ever. But this time, even I was afraid of him! It was like an angry, hungry bear waking up after a long hibernation. So many times I thought of doing something to her, but every time I thought about it, my children's faces would come to my mind. I knew that I had to get away before I did something that I couldn't undo.

Lucky for me, some orders came down the pike for me to go to Japan. I knew that I would be gone for a year, and maybe by the time I came back home, I could have rocked the monster back to sleep. I am torn between the family man that I was so long to be and the monster that hungers for souls. I always knew this war was waging inside me. Which part of the man that I am will be victorious?

# THE TWIN TOWERS

SEPTEMBER 11, 2001, WAS A HORRIBLE DAY for most of our American citizens. I remember being awakened by the ringing of the telephone at a very early hour in the morning, about 1:30–2:30 a.m. On the other end of the phone was the voice of my platoon commander yelling into the phone for me to wake up and turn on the news. He said, "The Twin Towers were attacked by terrorists!" I was stationed in Japan, so the time difference is why it was so early in the morning. I remember wiping the sleep from my eyes and turning on the news to see them replaying the planes flying into the towers. When I first saw it, I was in shock, like so many other Americans. After the shock went away, I felt anger from my toes to the top of my head. I started to cry.

Not from being sad, but from the anger that I felt inside of me. I got dressed to go for a run to sooth my mind, but as I looked out the window, I saw that we were in the middle of tropical storm Nari, with winds reaching 85 miles per hour. But strangely, I then felt a little excitement because I knew that this act by terrorists would not go unpunished. Or at least I hoped it wouldn't. That meant that I was going back to war. I no longer worried about rocking the monster back to sleep; instead, I could feed him. The battle continues…

On October 7, 2001, President George W. Bush announced the start of Operation Enduring Freedom at that time; he also confirmed air strikes that were taking place in Afghanistan. The funny thing is that on September 16, 2001, my wish came true about going to war because my unit was on an airplane on our way to a country neighboring, Afghanistan. Just five short days after 9/11, we were on our way. That may seem like a short time, but for us, it wasn't. We always had what is called a war bag (a bag carrying all the equipment you need when deploying that will sustain you for several days) at the ready.

My unit had to be ready to deploy (move troops or equipment into position for military action) within forty-eight hours to any place in the world. When the United States invaded Afghanistan, the mission was to dismantle al-Qaeda and to deny the Taliban a safe base of operations in Afghanistan. The Taliban controlled 90 percent of the country, so that tells you that we had a big job ahead of us.

Our first mission was in Kandahar. This was a fucked-up place to be in. I remember from the moment that we hit the ground, we had rounds zipping past our heads. When this happens, you do one of two things: fire back or freeze. Even if you don't know where they are coming from, you just fire in the direction that you think you're taking fire from. It was the private next to me that froze stiff, almost like he was playing that game we all played as kids, freeze tag. The only thing is that if he got tagged, then the game was over for him permanently.

A few rounds hit the dirt in front of the private, and he still did not move! I got up, ran over to him, and tackled him as if we were in the NFL, and I was a middle linebacker breaking through the lines and hitting a quarterback. It was a hard hit. My old coach would have been proud. That hit knocked the breath out of him. Even after that hard hit, he was still in a daze. I smacked him a few times, calling his name, then he snapped out of it. I was yelling at him to fire his weapon! Before I knew it, he was in the fight. As he was firing his weapon, he looked over at me and asked what kind of weapon they were using.

I smiled, and all I could think was in the movie *Heartbreak Ridge* when Gunny Highway said, "This is the AK47 assault rifle, the preferred weapon of your enemy. It makes a very distinctive sound when fired at you, so remember it." After I said that in my best Gunny Highway voice, I started to laugh. I'm sure that private thought that it was something wrong with me laughing in the middle of what was going on around us. I told him to get used to hearing that sound and not to be afraid of it. But to be very afraid when he can no longer hear that sound because that means that he's dead. Again, I started to laugh, then gave the private a wink and told him to keep shooting. Just sitting here talking about it, I can smell that place. I can actually taste the air in my mouth. I can even hear the rounds zipping past my head. When I close my eyes, I can see the burned-up vehicles and blown-up buildings.

My unit was pulled from Kandahar and sent to Jalalabad. This place was worse than the other place that we were at. I spent eighteen months in that country and loved every minute of it. Every time we went out on patrol, I got excited, hoping we might get into a firefight. To me, that was better than sex. That may sound crazy to you, but that was such a rush. Everyone knew that if you did not want to go outside the wire, don't ask to be on my team. (Leaving base camp) I would ask to take as many missions as I could outside the wire. The more you went outside the wire, the better your chances of being killed. Understand, it's not like I had a death wish. (So I thought.)

After eighteen months, we got our orders to go home. Instead of going back to Japan, we went back to the States. I was sad to leave the action behind but excited to see my kids and even my wife. After coming back to the States, I got stationed in Ohio, the state that I'm from. I was lucky enough to be stationed at a reserve unit that was about forty-five minutes from the place where my wife had grown up. The office staff in a reserve unit is on active duty. The reservist only trains one weekend a month and two weeks a year, but between those times they have questions and issues that may come up and need someone to help them with. As much as I enjoyed being home with my family, I still couldn't get that place out of my mind.

It almost felt like I was leaving an old girlfriend behind, with the thought of never seeing her again. That old girlfriend that you knew wasn't good for you, but you also knew that you would always love and miss her. I knew that I needed to try to focus on what was in front of me. I needed to focus on keeping the monster under control.

Sometimes I would think about that place, and it would bring a smile to my face, and other times it would piss me off. I could not understand why that was. It was confusing to me. How can the same thing bring you both joy and sadness? I also felt myself becoming explosive over some of the smallest things. It was never turned on by my family, but everyone outside of my home was open game.

I can recall one time when my family and I were in the van going to the store. As we were driving through the parking lot, a truck cut us off. My wife looked at me and said, "David, let it go." I looked at her and said that he could have killed you guys. She said, "Yes, he could have, but he didn't." I followed him till he parked, then I jumped out of the van before it came to a full stop. My wife had put the van in park to stop it. I ran over to his truck, leaned inside his truck window, and asked him what the hell his fucking problem was. I said you almost killed my family and pulled him through the window of his truck.

I started to bang him against the side of his truck. I can't remember if I was saying anything to him as I was doing that, because everything went black. My wife was yelling for me to let him go. I could hear her, but I couldn't understand what she was saying. It was almost like she was miles away. I didn't snap out of it until I heard my kids crying and saying, Daddy, please stop! I just looked at the guy and said that I'm sorry for what happened. He also said that he was sorry for cutting us off. He went over to my van and told my family that he was sorry for scaring them. I shook the guy's hand and again told him that I was sorry. When I got back in the van, my family was looking at me as if they were looking at a scary movie on TV. I didn't know what to say to them other than, "How about we go get some ice cream?" That helped with the kids, but not so much with my wife.

My wife told me that we needed to talk when we got home. I could tell, by the way she said it, that it wasn't going to be something pleasant. When we got home, she sent the kids outside to play. She looked at me and asked what the hell was that in the parking lot today. I looked at her and said that I was not sure why I did; that it just came out. She told me that I needed to do something about my anger problems. I told her that I don't have anger problems, then got mad and walked out of the house to go for a ride before I exploded.

I went to a bar down the street from my house to have a drink and calm down. As I'm having my drink, some drunken ass bumps into me and knock my drink off the bar. I looked at him and could feel the monster starting to awaken. I was trying really hard to keep him from coming out. It's almost like when Bruce Banner is trying to keep the Hulk at bay. The guy looked at me and said, "What the fuck are you looking at, nigger?"

I stepped down off my bar stool and said, "I'm sorry, I didn't hear what you said." As he started to say it again, I hit him so quick and hard in the mouth that his front tooth was stuck in the knuckle of my right hand. He dropped to the floor like a sack of potatoes. His eyes were open, but you could tell that he was out cold. His body was as stiff as a board with his arms in the air. I pulled the tooth from my hand and went wild in the bar, yelling, "Who is next?" Who wants to step up and take on the champ? No one was willing to do so. The guy that I hit was still out cold on the floor. As I was walking out of the bar, I just kept asking why people must make me do those things.

I try to do right, but they won't let me do the right thing. After driving around in my car, my hand really started to hurt. I looked down, and I had a hole in my hand that was two times bigger than it should have been and was bleeding. I thought that I couldn't go back home because my wife would say something about my anger problems, and that was the last thing that I wanted to hear.

So I went to the ER and had my knuckle looked at. The doctor asked me how it happened. I told him that I hit someone, and his tooth got stuck in my hand. He started to tell me how many germs and bacteria are in a human's mouth. I looked at the doctor and said, "Doc, I'm not trying to be an ass, but can you just stitch it up or whatever you're going to do and not talk to me anymore." He looked at me like he wanted to say something but was afraid that one of his teeth would be stuck in my other hand.

The doctor was a short, little, round guy, so I'm sure the last thing that he wanted was for me to get pissed off and take a swing at him. Or maybe he was thinking that he wished that he was stitching up the hand of the other guy after hitting me in the mouth. Whatever he was thinking didn't matter to me. All I could think about was what I was going to tell my wife when I got home. The doctor cleaned my hand and put a few stitches in it, then sent me home. Of course, I didn't go straight home. I went to a different bar to have a drink and figure out the story that I was going to tell my wife, especially because we had just talked about my aggressive and explosive temper.

As I sat there, I had to wonder to myself, could she be right? Am I out of control? After thinking about that question, I came up with: I do the things that I do because people force me to do them. If people would just leave me alone, then I wouldn't have to act the way that I do.

I finished my drink and headed home to face the music. When I got home, she asked why my hand was bandaged up. I simply told her about my friend. I was helping to fix his car and slammed my knuckles, trying to get a bolt undone. She just looked at me as if she knew that wasn't the truth, but she didn't say anything to me and just kept doing what she was doing. A few days later, she said that she had been doing some reading, and it was about Post-Traumatic Stress Disorder (PTSD), and that she thinks that I may be suffering from that and that I should go and see someone. I told her that PTSD is not real. Pussies that are afraid to go and do the job that they said they would do on the day that they raised their right hand and swore to defend this country uses that for an excuse.

Not only that, but also even if it were real, only weak-minded guys would get it, and by far, I was not a weak-minded guy. How can you be weak-minded and still go to combat and love it? How can you pull the trigger and not regret it when the round leaves the chamber? Not only were those guys weak-minded, but they were also bitches. I don't recall that being one of the things that they taught us in boot camp, ***how to be a bitch***. You are a Marine, for god's sake! Grow a pair of nuts, then reach down and grab them. Do your freaking job. Am I in denial? Is my monster winning this war or just the battle? Am I the reason my relationships fail?

# Back to Japan

About a month after the bar fight, I received orders to go back to Japan. I could have taken my family with me, and I would have had to stay for three years or go alone and only go for one year. I chose to go for one year. I needed time away from my wife, and I think that she also needed time away from me. I felt that if I hadn't gone away, we may not have lasted much longer. A month after I got my orders, I was on an airplane back to the rock (Japan). I have to say that I was sad to leave my kids but glad to leave my wife.

When my plane landed in Japan, it felt like a weight had been lifted off my chest. It was like I could breathe again. This time, when I went back to Japan, I was an E6 (Staff Sergeant). The good thing about that was that I didn't have to live on base and could live out in town. I had a very small place. It was a one-room place. The kitchen, living room, and bedroom were all one room, followed by the bathroom. Like I said, it was a very small place, but it was all I needed.

When you're in Japan, you either become a runner, weightlifter, an alcoholic, or a born-again Christian. I merged the weightlifter and the alcoholic together. I think in that year that I was in Japan, I drank more and worked out more than I ever have in my entire life. It was nothing for me to be out all night drinking and get back just in time to change into my physical training (PT) uniform and run five miles with my unit. I would promise myself that I'm not going to do that again. That promise would last until I did the same thing again the next weekend. I spent a lot of time in the gym, and when I wasn't in the gym, I was out drinking.

Not sure how I could do both and live to tell about it. I do know that I was the strongest I had ever been. By the time I left Japan, I was bench pressing about 485 lbs. three times in a row. I'm sure some of that was because I was back on the juice. When they did a piss test back then, it was just for drugs, and besides, that wasn't a drug; it was an enhancer. Kind of like saying weed is not a drug; it's just a plant. After being in Japan for about six months, I put on another stripe. Now I am a Gunnery Sergeant (E7). I knew that I could not wait to go home before I drank myself to death. When it was time for me to leave Japan and return to the States, my family and I went to North Carolina. Shortly after I got back to my unit, there was talk that we were going to go to war in Iraq.

On March 5, 2003, my unit was activated and was given forty-eight hours to make sure all of our affairs were in order. When they told us to get our affairs in order, we knew that we were about to leave. I went home and told my wife that I was getting deployed. She was upset and asked why I always had to go. I told her that this is what I do for a living. I told her that she knew who I was when she married me. Plus, you didn't complain when you were picking out that new car that you drive or the checks that I get when I'm gone. (When you're in a combat zone, your checks are tax-free, plus you get extra pay. We got paid on the first and fifteenth of each month.) On March 8, we were on a plane heading someplace in the Middle East. It wasn't Iraq, but it was a place close to Iraq.

On March 19, the US began the invasion of Iraq. We sent satellite-guided Tomahawk cruise missile strikes on Baghdad. After the missile strikes, American, British, Australian, Polish, and Danish military operations began sending ground troops into Iraq. My unit was one of the units in the first wave. This brought me much joy to have this opportunity and pleasure to finally be able to feed that monster inside of me again. You could tell that it had been a long time, and he was ready to feed. The feeling that came over me just thinking about what was about to happen was better than any sexual fantasy that I could have ever had. (Thinking back on how I felt almost makes me ashamed to tell the rest of this story.)

On April 3, the First Mar Div (First Marin Division) and Task Force Tarawa were moving on to Baghdad from the southwest. They expected us to face heavy resistance along the way. We were on standby to re-enforce the Fifth Marine Division. When the Fifth Marines got to Route six near Al Aziziyah, they came against the Republican Guard troops, Saddam Fedayeen, and foreign volunteers from other close by countries like Syria, Egypt, and other close by countries that are allies. It's always nice to be stabbed in the back by so-called allies. This turned out to be one of the fiercest engagements of the war.

As the Intel was coming in, it was hard to listen to what was happening because we could hear the engagement in real time. We were able to just imagine the casualties that were coming along with the forward movement of the Fifth Marines. I know this next thing that I'm about to say may be hard for you to understand, but I felt a bit of excitement listening to the Intel. I know that sounds bad, but I knew the worse it got, the better the chances of me getting to suit up, so to speak, it was almost like a football player sitting on the sidelines waiting for the coach to put him in the game. The coach looked over and told us to get in the game. We joined the Fifth Marines after they made it across the Diyala River.

After our mission was over, we went back to North Carolina. About eight months later, we went back for a second time. This time, when we went back, it was different. It's hard to explain what I mean by different. Almost as if I wasn't sure what I was doing there. Before, some of the things that I did or saw didn't bother me. Sometimes I felt myself starting to hesitate in some of my thoughts. That was frightening because that could get someone hurt or even killed. You don't always have time to think. You just have to do it and think about it later, when time presents itself.

That was the other problem; I hated having that time to think. My mind would be all over the place. I could not keep my thoughts straight. I felt that it was starting to get dangerous; I couldn't stay focused on anything that I was doing! I would forget what I was doing and would stand up and look around, hoping that I would see something to remind me of what I was doing. I'm not sure, but I felt like the people around me could tell that I was off my game.

I wasn't sleeping, and I wasn't eating. What put me over the edge was the night the car drove through the checkpoint. That night, I was checking on my guys at the front gate when a car was driving like a madman coming up at the front gate. I told the person on the 50 cal. to put a few rounds in front of the car to slow it down. He did, but the car kept coming. I told him to stop the car; normally, that means to shoot the engine block with the 50 cal. He put about five rounds in the car and stopped it. We went out of the gate to check on the car. When we got to the car and looked, I saw a man and his little girl bleeding out. Not only did he stop the car, but he also killed the man and little girl.

The only thing that I could think was that she was about the same age as my youngest daughter. That really messed me up. For the first time ever, I wanted to go home. When I was alone sometimes I would just start crying for no reason no one could know that would cry because they would no longer trust my orders, and that wouldn't be good for any of us. The day the order came down that we were going home was one of the best days of my life.

WHEN I GOT HOME, THINGS JUST DIDN'T feel right! The nightmares started to wake me up in the middle of the night. I would wake up in cold sweats; other times my wife would wake me up because I was yelling in my sleep. It got to the point that she would sleep on the couch because she was frightened to sleep in the same bed with me. It was getting harder and harder every day to get out of bed. When I did get out of bed, the only way that I felt normal was when I was drinking, smoking weed, or taking pills that I got from a friend. The longer this went on, the more I had to do to feel normal (whatever normal is).

I felt like my world was spinning out of control. Even my kids, who are my pride and joy, couldn't make me happy. I didn't want to spend time with them. I started to have thoughts that I was better off dead! Many times I would ask why I made it home and not some of the guys that didn't. (I didn't know at the time, but that is called survivors guilt.) I would see the faces of guys that I saw lying on the ground and thinking they were someone's husband, father, brother, son, and uncle. Someone out there was crying to see them again and never will.

I started to take unsafe risks. I didn't care what happened to me. Everyone around me would tell me that I needed to go and talk to someone about how I was feeling. I didn't think that anyone could or would understand how I felt. I was pretty sure that I was the only one who had these feelings. How could anyone else feel what I felt? They weren't with me. They didn't see what I saw. They didn't do the things that I did. So how could they possibly understand what I was feeling? I didn't think that things were as bad as they were until I tried to kill myself—not just once, but twice. I won't get into the details of how. That's when I knew that things were past the point of no return.

I made an appointment to go see someone. Sometimes dealing with the military on things takes a little time; it took about three days to see a doctor. He was a military doctor, so I felt that he should be able to fix me. I didn't know that I wasn't broken; I was just hurting. The night before my doctor's appointment, I couldn't sleep because I was afraid that he or she was going to tell me that I was crazy. I knew that I wasn't crazy, even if I felt like I was going crazy! All I could think about was in the movies when someone in the military so-called went crazy (Section 8). They were put in a hospital and pumped full of drugs till they were drooling from the mouth, and then put out of the military.

Then they are living on the streets, talking to themselves. Now I'm sitting outside the doctor's office, waiting to be seen. The door opened, and the doctor asked me to come into his office. So before he could say anything, I started off by saying, I'm not crazy. He looked at me and asked why I started with that. He then asked me if I thought that I was crazy. I jumped up and said, "Hell no, I'm not crazy." I just wanted to put that out there before you try to say that I am crazy. He asked me if I was trying to convince him that I'm not crazy or convince myself that I'm not crazy. He could tell that I started to get pissed. Thinking back, I'm really not sure why I was getting pissed off.

He asked me to sit back down so that we could talk about what was bothering me. I sat down, and he started to ask me questions about some of the things that were going on with me. Things were going well until he said, "I understand." When he said that, something inside of me went off like a firecracker. To this day, I am not sure why it did. I asked the doctor if he had ever been in combat, and he said no. Then he started with, "But I do." I jumped up, and he stopped midsentence. I then yelled, "If you have never been in combat, then how can you say that you understand?

You can never understand something that you have never experienced!" I told him that he was a freaking waste of time to talk to and then stormed out of his office. That's when I knew that I was on my own with this because I'm the only person in the world who knew what I was dealing with. Unfortunately, at the time, I did not know that I wasn't alone in the way that I was feeling.

I dealt with these problems the best way that I could for the next few years. Each day, I had to talk myself off the ledge so that I wouldn't jump off. So now I'm retiring from the Marines, and in my head, I'm still broken. The only thing I can think about now is what I am going to do with the rest of my life. How much harder it will be to deal with my problems because I couldn't talk to regular people about some of the things that were on my mind because they definitely wouldn't understand.

By now, my wife was done with it or me. She never really understood what I was dealing with. To her, it was all about what it was doing to her. What was it doing to her? What about what it was doing to me? I was mad because I felt that she should have been trying harder to help me. I'm not sure what I wanted her to help me with, but I knew that I wanted her to try. I felt that she gave up on me; she didn't have my six. How could she have left me out in the cold all alone? Looking back in her head, she probably thought that she did try to help and that I didn't want or need her help.

On our anniversary, her birthday, the house of cards that I was living in came crashing down around me. She told me that she was done and wanted out. I was in shock and asked her what she meant by wanting out. She looked at me and said, "What parts do you not get? I want out of this marriage."

I looked at her and said, "I know things haven't been perfect, but I didn't think that they were that bad."

She laughed and said, "Perfect, that is a funny joke!" She said that if I had used the word "good," then she would still have laughed, but just not as hard. I asked her how she could do this on our anniversary. She said that she did not do this on our anniversary; she did this on her birthday. She told me that the best gift that I could give her for her birthday was a new life without me in it.

I was crushed. I had to sit down in a chair before I fell to the floor. I felt my legs go weak, and I almost didn't make it to the chair. In all the fights that I've been in, I've never been hit that hard before. She almost knocked me out without ever throwing a punch. I asked her, "So what does this mean for our family, our kids?" She said that our kids are still our kids, but as far as our family, it's over.

That night, after the kids went to bed, I left my/our home. I learned a lesson that night, and the lesson was that if you plan on leaving, have a place to go before you leave. I know it sounds funny, but when I left, I got in my car, got to the end of my street, and thought I had no place to go. I couldn't go back home because that would have been a blow to my manhood to ask her if I could stay because I had no place to go. So I sat at the corner of my street for a minute, crying and thinking about what's next. I felt like I had lost my career, family, and will to live. I got myself together, called a friend, and asked him if I could stay with him and his family for a few days.

I kind of told him what was going on, and he said that I could stay. He asked me how long it would be till I got to his house, and I said, "Look out the window." He just started laughing and said the door was unlocked. That was a long night, because I had no idea what the next day would have in store for me. Jessy (my friend) sat up with me the rest of the night, talking to me. I could tell that he was worried about me. He was worried about what I may do to myself. Not that I don't blame him, because if things had been the other way around, I would have been worried too. I'm sure he was thinking, *if he left me alone, what would his family have woken up to?* I know that seems a bit extreme.

My thoughts that night were extreme. The next morning, all I could think was everything that I knew, as my life was no more. I was no longer a Marine, no longer a husband, no longer a father, and no longer a man. Now I know that I was wrong in the way that I was thinking. Once a Marine, always a Marine. I may have no longer been a husband, but I was **still** a **father** and a **man**. The only thing that I could think about was how and what would I tell the kids. After giving it a lot of thought, I went back to my house to talk with my wife. Thinking that she had time to cool off and that she would not want the divorce.

I was wrong; she still wanted the divorce, and she wasn't upset, just fed up. No matter how much I begged and pleaded for her not to take my family away, it did not help. She told me to take what I needed and to leave her house. I packed a bag and asked her if I could come back over when the kids got home from school so that I could tell them bye. She said that she would think about it and call me later to let me know. After a few hours, I called her to tell her that I was on my way over so that we could talk.

When I got to the house, she said that she had nothing more to say and that our marriage was over. I said that was fine, but we needed to talk about the kids. I told her that she could keep the house, and I would continue to pay the mortgage and the rest of the bills. Deep down, I knew that she had someone else, no matter how much she said that she didn't.

For the next few months, we did not tell the kids that we had split up. I would come over in the morning before the kids woke up for school, and I would leave to go home after they went to bed. I moved from Jessy's house and found a house close by so that I could see the kids. Jessy got me a job working with him at a car dealership. I went from being a combat Marine to a car salesman. What's even crazier is that I was good at it! I did that for a few years, and I made a good living doing it. The only thing is that I was not fulfilled doing that kind of work. I bounced around, doing different jobs. I worked in the prison system. I went from being a correction officer to a lieutenant in charge of the Special Tactical Response Team, and after doing that for a few years, I also left that job.

I felt it would be best to leave that job before I ended up in prison myself. I came to that conclusion after my third federal "excessive use of force" committee hearing. I knew that I couldn't be a police officer because I felt angry all the time and knew that wouldn't end well for me. I ended up a bouncer in nightclubs and enjoyed the nights that I got to break up fights because that way I could fight too.

I was well known to many club promoters and was always busy with work from them, doing private parties and club work. I enjoyed banging heads together, but after a while, that wasn't fun anymore. So from there, I worked as Regional Loss Prevention Manager for a major retailer. My losses at all of my stores were down. I would like to think it was because I put great policies in place. It wasn't; it was because I had an army of brutes working for me. That is the way that I liked it. If you were caught shoplifting in one of my stores and didn't get your ass beat, then the guys that stopped you were out of a job.

I trained my guys in hand-to-hand combat. You had training one day a week. You missed training; you were looking for a new job. If you were an employee from one of the stores and got caught stealing, you were fired on the spot, and a big deal was made of it. You did the walk of shame so that everyone in the store knew what you did. Plus, charges were pressed against you. It didn't matter if it was one dollar or one million dollars. After a while, I left that job. I could tell that my tactics were starting to become Gestapo-like.

No matter what kind of job I had, I just couldn't find happiness. The only time that I felt like I had any happiness was when I was bringing pain to someone. I believe it was that monster that lived inside of me. After leaving the Marines, I had no real way to feed him. It got to the point that many thoughts that I had were not good.

One time I sat on my couch with a shotgun in my mouth, and another time I had my pistol in my mouth. Each time when I had the courage to pull the trigger, someone stopped me. They either called or came over. To this day, those two people have no idea that they saved my life. I was afraid to be alone because, in the quiet, my thoughts were so loud that I felt like I was going crazy. I hated to leave my house because I never knew how my day would go. Large crowds made me angry for no reason. I mean angry to the point that I wanted to hurt someone. Also, around this time, I met a woman named Victoria.

Shortly after Victoria and I got together, I got custody of my son, David. Annie's boyfriend didn't want David around and made it clear by the way that he treated him. One day, David called me crying, asking if he could live with me. After getting him to calm down, I asked him what was wrong. He told me that his mom's boyfriend cusses at him and bullies him. That was all I needed to hear to wake the monster up. I lived about fifteen minutes away and made it to her house in five minutes. She must have known that I was on my way because he was gone before I got to the house. Looking back, I'm glad that he was. I'm not sure whether or not I would have killed him if he were still there.

# The Reset Button

Time to hit the reset button! If only it were that easy, and all you had to do was hit reset and start over. I now not only have to keep it together for myself, but also now I have my son to hold it together for. Life is really moving about a hundred miles an hour, and the curves in the road are getting harder to see. As a single dad and in a new relationship, I could feel my life starting to spin out of control. I was so afraid that I would screw my son up! I felt that I was screwed up! I felt like I was out in the middle of the ocean. I could see the land, but I felt that I was too far away to swim to it. But I knew that I had to try and swim to shore, if not for me, but for my son. I knew that I needed to get some help, but I did not know where to go to get the help that I needed. Heck, I didn't even know what kind of help I needed.

My older brother, Jimmy, was also retired from the military. He retired from the Air Force, and his job in the Air Force was as a mental health technician. One day, I called Jimmy crying, asking him to help me. I knew that he would be able to help point me to someone who could help. It took him a little bit to calm me down enough to understand what I wanted. The problem was that I lived in one state and he loved in a different state, but he knew who to tell me to go see. He told me to call the local VA office and tell them that I was in the middle of a mental health crisis. Jimmy made me promise to call them as soon as we hung up the phone.

I promised him, then we hung up. Just like I promised, I called the VA office and told them what he told me to say. Someone talked to me on the phone for about an hour, then got me in to see someone the next day. That was the day that I pushed the reset button. Just because I pushed the reset button didn't mean that I didn't have to put in the work. This was something that was needed not only for me but also for everyone that I love. After working with my therapist, more and more things in my life made sense, both past and present. I was learning that anxiety and emotions are not always "monsters"! Traumatic experiences, whether from a young age or war-torn Marine, are very real.

I was better able to understand why I did many of the things that I did. I learned that I first had to change the way I think about things. One of the things that I also learned was that post-traumatic stress disorder (PTSD) is real and that I was suffering from it. PTSD is caused by a traumatic experience. I think that I may have had a touch of PTSD before joining the military, but it was worsened by my time in the military. Not just the military, but my time in combat. I did several tours in different combat zones. In those combat zones, I did and saw many things that are not normal and could be very traumatic. The thing is, at the time, I didn't realize just how traumatic those things were to me. Don't get me wrong, therapy was not easy, and there were many times I wanted to give up. It brought back many things that I had buried in my mind. We often do that to protect ourselves.

Was my monster part of a defense mechanism? Fight or flight— kill or be killed?

I knew that I couldn't give up on myself because that would mean that I was giving up on living. I have already traveled that road, and it is a lonely road to travel. Finally, things are going well. My son is doing well, and my relationship with Victoria is thriving. So by now, Victoria and I are living together, along with my son. We also moved from the state that we lived into the state that my brother,

Jimmy, lives in. Not only did we move to that state, but we also moved a street over from him and his family. My life is finally my life.

That same year, I went back to school to get my degree in counseling. I knew that there were a ton of vets who could use my help. At one time, I was in a very dark place and made it back. I knew that I had the road map to make it back and wanted to share it with others. A few times, however, I thought that I may have picked the wrong career because, many times, classwork would make me visit those dark places in my head that I thought I was done with. I have to send a huge thank you to Jimmy for pushing me to keep going. He reminded me of all the souls that I could save. That was huge to me because before I was so consumed with taking them, now I want to save them. This, at first, was a big internal conflict because that monster still lived inside of me.

Many nights, he and I would have it out. The more I worked on myself, the angrier he became. He knew that one day he would be given an eviction notice. That was scary for both of us. For me, because that means that I would become more vulnerable, and for him, because it would be the end of him. Becoming vulnerable was scary because what if someone saw that I was vulnerable? Would they take advantage of me? The monster would no longer be there to protect me. I soon learned that I did not need that monster to protect me! I could protect myself.

Not only did I learn that I could protect myself, but I also learned that I could teach others that they could protect themselves as well. Don't get me wrong; the monster is not gone. When I served him with eviction papers, he didn't leave; he just became tamed. I'm sure if the conditions were right, he would come out again. The trick is making sure that the conditions are never right for him to rear his ugly head. Maybe I am normal after all. Maybe the monster only lied to me repeatedly. Maybe now I realize I am stronger than any ugly monster.

I PUT MY TIME INTO SCHOOL, AND NOW I have graduated with my degree. That was a short-lived bit of excitement. I have my degree, but I had no idea what to do with it. All I knew was that I wanted to change the world. Wow! That is a huge statement. Change the world? What exactly does that mean—to change the world? After a few months of trying to figure it out, I took a job working as a substance abuse counselor. I enjoyed the work, but not the company that I worked for. This company was more into it for the money than helping people. They had a government contract with the Department of Corrections. So to them, it was all about getting bodies in the door. They would say people needed treatment. They didn't really need treatment just to get paid for the contract.

They knew that those people had no choice but to come, or many of them would go back to jail. I felt bad for some of the clients, because if they didn't comply with the treatment recommended, needed, or not, they would go back to jail. Plus, many of the counselors were not certified to work there. I worked with that company for a few years, then moved on to be the director of a veteran transitional facility. I really enjoyed doing this work. The state that I lived in had a high homeless population, with many of those being veterans. The hot weather year-round made it easier to be homeless.

Whenever a homeless veteran came out of the woods and wanted to start over, I was able to help them. It put a smile on my face. It also gave a purpose to life. Without a purpose to life, it's hard to live. I've been there, and I never want to go back.

This job made it so that I was able to share the road map that I used to make it back from that very dark place. Whenever I said to a veteran that I understood, he or she knew that I did understand and wasn't just saying that I did. I made sure that they knew that I had been in the same shoes that many of them had been in. The slogan "Leave no service member behind," I lived that. I would go out in the woods to the homeless camps looking for service members, hoping that I could talk them into coming out of the woods and seeking help. Many times they weren't ready to leave the woods, but they would come to my office to see what kind of help was out there when they were ready for it.

Some would come to my office just to talk or to get a hot meal. Whatever the reason they came for, they knew that my door was always open to them. That job, other than being a Marine, was one of the most satisfying jobs I have ever had. But the most satisfying job I had, by far, was being a father.

I did this job for many years before leaving to become a partner in my own private practice. I am proud to say that I was instrumental in helping over one thousand veterans and family members. From things such as providing a hot meal or putting a roof over their heads before leaving that position. A person that I worked with as a substance abuse counselor already had her own small private practice on the side. I talked her into doing it full-time instead of part-time. It was a mental health substance abuse counseling office. I so enjoyed working in my own private practice because I was able to do things my way. That made it easier to help those who needed it.

Working as a counselor and helping others has also helped me. I don't try to fool myself into thinking that he is gone, because he isn't gone, just controlled. I have also helped others, not just veterans, to control the monster in their lives. It took a long time to learn how to control that monster. I know that it is something that I must take inventory of on a daily basis. I know that he is just waiting for me to let my guard down and catch me slipping, and he will come back with a vengeance.

I sold my half of the practice to my partner and set out on this journey to tell my story in hopes that someone would read it and that it might help them on their journey in life. As of the time that I am writing this book, on average, twenty-two veterans a day are taking their own lives. With any hope, maybe just one of those veterans who are thinking about ending their lives will read my story and know that they are not alone. There is hope and help for you, but you have to take the first step and ask for it. There is no shame in asking for help.

Go online to VA.gov or call 1-800-827-1000, and remember that your sacrifices are appreciated. That is for combat and noncombat veterans, because we have all made sacrifices when putting on that uniform, no matter what uniform you wore or wear.

# About the Author

Desmond A. Cook is a retired military veteran with twenty years of dedicated service. Throughout his career, he was awarded several medals and ribbons. He also rose to the rank of first sergeant at retirement. Desmond currently resides in Georgia with his wife and beloved dog. *A Broken Mind of a Marine* is his first book.